For Mom and Dad

Slower Style – The Amazing Future of Sustainable Fashion

Table of Contents

Slower Style – The Amazing Future of Sustainable Fashion

Introduction

Sustainability is Balance

Slower Style – The Amazing Future of Sustainable Fashion

Sustainability is Balance

I like when words have meaning.

Maybe you've once heard of someone who is afraid of making the wrong impression, so they use complex words to get their ideas across. A real-life enactment of Mr. Collins, from Pride and Prejudice may come to mind. Somehow, you've been teleported back to a time when the only way to assert authority is through the use of big words.

The times have changed, and so has the way we talk.

Sustainably is no different. There is a host of people who try to assert themselves as experts in something they know nothing about. Buzzwords of "net zero," and "energy efficient" are thrown around like candy, and their audiences are left with this vague sense of confusion and resentment.

That's all about to change. Through the course of this book, I plan on sharing the true meaning of sustainability through the fashion industry. As the second largest polluter, next to big oil, the fashion industry is due for a much-needed overhaul.

We're going to walk through what it means to be a more thoughtful consumer. You will have the tools to turn a messy closet into a chic, clean, and sustainable wardrobe. If you're really ambitious, you may feel even motivated to start your own sustainable fashion line.

Slower style is the antithesis to fast fashion. Slowing down the turnover rate of your closet, spending more time to make the garments, higher quality, and affordable prices is the world you are about to enter. How exciting!

Sustainability is the Balance between The Environment, The Economy, and Social Justice

See, many people have these misconceptions about genuine sustainability because we keep getting stuck listening to people who have no idea of what they are talking about. Yes, there are major benefits to businesses, governments, and communities that invest in hiring sustainability professionals. However, without knowing what you're looking for it is very difficult to do so.

That's why I'm trying to fix this misconception... one word at a time.

Yes, I have a degree in Sustainability from one of the best Universities of Sustainability in the world. I personally believe that my degree is utterly worthless unless I can use them to communicate correctly about sustainability with those who don't have the degrees.

If you can't explain it to a six-year-old,
you don't understand it yourself

This book exists to relate some complicated and vague concepts about sustainability to the people who need it the most: The rest of us. I love writing about sustainability in food, beauty, fashion, and environmental health because I feel very close to those topics and don't believe they get enough credit in our STEM-focused sustainability culture.

Science and math are essential in understanding the broad energy and resource crises. Most of us will never use these concepts in our everyday lives (contrary to what my professors say). I'd rather talk about all the other things that seem to be getting lost in a frenzy towards renewable energy and solving climate change.

I like to write about fashion and beauty within sustainability because no one seems to be giving them enough attention when the fashion industry globally makes up 1.2 trillion dollars of the GDP. I started my sustainable clothing brand, Bottle Thread to help reduce plastic waste while producing top quality, ethically sourced garments.

Focus on the Topics You Love with the People You Care Most About

Climate change is still impacting our globe today, and sustainable technology is here to fix that. Though, I prefer

Slower Style – The Amazing Future of Sustainable Fashion

to do so without using the icky-gross buzz words that consultants always keep thinking are okay to use. Let's cut the nonsense, and get the facts straight. We only have one Earth, and we shouldn't waste it with all this confusion.

Sustainability doesn't start with impressive technology. It begins with knowledge, and I work to make it understandable for you as possible.

How I made a Profitable, Sustainable Business before I graduated

Even though I support focusing on getting a job after college through paid internships and extra circular activities, it isn't the path for everyone. Early on, I recognized that I would not be able to succeed in the 9–5 atmosphere that awaited most of my friends after graduation.

I have an invisible disability called Multiple Chemical Sensitivity (MCS), where it has made it close to impossible to be a reliable employee in the corporate world.

If you met me in person, you might not ever know how exposure to perfume and other everyday household products leave me with excruciating migraines. Very often, I would have to go home early and miss the rest of the day of paid work. People felt resentful, and my schedule was unpredictable. It was a nightmare, to be honest.

I ended up founding Bottle Thread: Sustainable shirts for women, made in America, out of recycled plastic bottles. So far, it has been a success. Though, I wouldn't have been able to start it without the resources and knowledge from my undergraduate degree at Chatham.

Don't follow your passion!

Most people don't expect this advice. Contrary to popular belief, following your passion doesn't guarantee life satisfaction or happiness. Instead, follow your talent and MAKE it your passion.

If someone told my 15-year-old self that I would be running a successful sustainable fashion company at 22, I'd have laughed them out of the room. To put it mildly, I was a punk-goth kid with short-pixie hair, studded belts and an obsession with hard-core metal bands. Fashion seemed frivolous, and the word "sustainability" didn't exist.

When I started brainstorming ideas for business, I wanted to focus on a problem that impacted a lot of people. At the time, I was wearing a great quality polyester button-down shirt that fit me perfectly. This shirt was the only button down shirt that ever actually fit me, and I couldn't find a replacement ANYWHERE.

I was also learning about sustainable waste disposal at the time and was appalled at some plastic bottles we threw out every year. Once the two ideas were connected, I knew I had a viable product. Though, if I followed my passion, I would have gotten burned out.

Passion doesn't always meet people's needs, but meeting needs can become a passion.

Utilize your Resources when you Have Them

I have yet to find a college metric for aspiring entrepreneurs outside of the things you learn in class. Most schools focus on the curriculum, extracurricular activities, and networking when it comes to business majors. I wasn't a business major, nor wanted to be a business major, and there didn't seem to be a place where I could do business networking if I weren't a business major; until I went to Chatham.

On a whim, I took this class in database management with Dr. Chung at Chatham. Why? I don't know. It just looked interesting. Though, throughout the class and afterward, I made a real networking connection with my professor which would significantly impact my college experience.

Dr. Chung connected me with the Women's Center for Business and Entrepreneurship. I would be invited to mixers, workshops, and meet-ups throughout the city. I'd have access to incubator programs, mentors, and actual investors.

Many of these resources I would not have had access to, had it been I went somewhere else, chose a different major, or done anything differently.

If you are still in school and have the motivation to start on the path towards financial security before graduation, utilize the resources you have and meet a need that can become your passion. The rest will follow.

2017 - Frownfelter

Slower Style – The Amazing Future of Sustainable Fashion

Sustainable Fashion

How we can fix the world's second largest polluting industry

Slower Style – The Amazing Future of Sustainable Fashion

The Rise of Slower Style

Sustainable Fashion is a pretty simple yet not so simple concept. However, its upcoming Omnipresence in the industry is going to be for the 2020's as jeans were for the 1960's and beyond.

Sustainability by definition is not a trend. It is simply the balance between people, the planet, and making money.

But see it's a lot more complicated than that simply because there are many factors at play here. You have ethical fashion, cruelty-free fashion, practical fashion, minimalistic fashion, style over fashion, and even gluten-free jeans. People in the industry don't know what end is up, let alone everyone else.

Here, we dive a little into what sustainability means and how it applies to fashion.

Sustainable = Balanced

Sustainable fashion is all about balance. If you focused too much on one of the three at the expense of the others, you'd not be sustainable.

For the past century (and longer), the society as a whole has been focused entirely on economic incentives. This has naturally been a disaster because it oppresses people and exploits our planet's resources.

There is no singular solution to solving the world's problems, and no one individual can do it alone. It will take a society-wide effort to fix these problems. It just takes time, effort, and dedication to something greater than monetary gains.

I dedicated myself to sustainable fashion just because it was something that interested me greatly, and no one else I knew was focusing on it. Sustainability and sustainable fashion will happen in due time. The main factor that is up for debate is who is going to be at the forefront? Who will lose out?

Maintaining profit incentive without exploiting workers and communities

Sustainable fashion is just another commodity if you think of it from a business standpoint. People see value in fashion. They buy it, use it and sell it. Repeat cycle.

We will always need clothing. Our expression of ourselves is tied to our ego, and our egos love pretty things. It's nothing to be ashamed of. Fashion isn't going anywhere, and sustainable fashion is here to at least help reduce our impact.

We all hear about sweatshops in foreign countries. Nothing seems to get better in the world of mass-market clothing. We hear stories about Ivanka Trump's clothing line exposed for being linked to manufacturers that harm the rights of workers. There are news stories summarizing atrocities, without giving any suggestions on how to fix it. It doesn't seem to get any better.

And yet, on the other hand, we hear about how people like Emma Watson insisting on fair-wage workers to produce clothing for the beauty and the beast movie. There is hope. There are inspiring stories, and it's out there. We just have to find it, and we should support fair wages when we can.

Producing products while minimizing the extraction of non-renewable resources

Sustainable fashion wouldn't be sustainable if we didn't talk about the environment. It's hardly debatable that people are polluting the planet even though some might choose to argue about climate change. Pollution, though, is not going away, and it won't unless we try to do something about it.

Except there is a weird distortion on why and the way we view pollution and responsibility. Some businesses cough up until this point have been profiting on solving problems that they create in the first place.

Slower Style – The Amazing Future of Sustainable Fashion

Pollution is one of them. If only, people polluted less, maybe we will have a chance at saving the planet. Except for that way of thinking is flawed.

We Can't Shop Our Way out of Climate Change, but we Can't Do Nothing Either.

Even if we were each able to correctly choose the right products that "help the environment" we still wouldn't be doing much of a dent on fixing them because these big problems require collective action. This is not something we can buy ourselves out of, except for that way of thinking is also a little bit flawed.

We can't just do nothing and hope that the collective action will somehow save us. The demand shifts when we buy different products. Therefore if you can reduce your pollution, and use a product that is mildly more helpful for the environment, over time, the markets will shift to produce better products.

That's where sustainable fashion comes into play:

By shifting trends over time, sustainable fashion has a chance at making a major impact on how we view and purchase clothing.

If we all practiced a little bit of mindfulness, we should be able to shift purchasing behavior and in turn the industry. It might not be a lot for now, but it's something. Years from now, we are going to look back on this decade as the time that more sustainable products started picking up steam in the mainstream. I want to be a part of that movement and hope you do too. That's why we're here to help you understand the planet's problems, and somehow make the planet a little greener.

The Green Fashion Myth

Sustainable fashion is eco-friendly, but eco-friendly fashion is not always sustainable. A lot of people seem to keep using the two interchangeably.

Eco Friendly Fashion is a sub-category of Sustainability

Many times I see the words eco-friendly and sustainable in the same advertisement. Let's set the record straight, if a product is truly sustainable, it is by default, eco-friendly. The same is not true, the other way around.

Sustainability is the balancing combination between the environment, ethics, and the economy.

Eco-friendly fashion may be better for the planet than typical fast fashion, but it does not make it sustainable. If a child slave made a garment with 100% organic cotton in a carbon-neutral factory, it is still unsustainable. Truly sustainable fashion can balance worker's rights with affordability to make eco-friendly fashion. Therefore, eco-friendly can be a subcategory of sustainability, but not the other way around. The two are NOT equal terms.

Green is not always Ethical

There has been a huge push for greener products in the last decade. The demand for eco-friendly fashion has increased just the same. However, green in fashion is not always ethical. Therefore green is not always sustainable.

Truly sustainable fashion will happen when we can incorporate the environment, ethics, and affordability into the same products. I'm putting together an ultimate list of sustainable fashion brands with a three-factor metric to figure out which ones are better at some things than others.

Given our way of life at the moment, it is tough to create truly sustainable fashion. The world is so entrenched in itself that it is difficult and practically impossible to separate products based on how sustainable they are. However, it is a good thing to get into the habit, as a conscious consumer, to look into the kinds of things you're buying. Green is not always Ethical, therefore not always sustainable.

Environmentally friendly is not always Affordable

The relatively good thing about fast fashion is how affordable it is to consumers. There is also relative ease in getting your hands on a cheap item of clothing. Going out of your way to buy something more sustainable is usually a lot more difficult and often costs more.

Just because a product is labeled as environmentally friendly, or made from an eco-friendly source, does not make it affordable and therefore does not make it sustainable. Ethical and Eco-Friendly Products are not always affordable, but truly sustainable fashion ethical, eco-friendly, and affordable.

Affordability is by far the most challenging part of sustainable fashion. However, it is because of something called path dependency. A rabbit trail turns into a footpath which turns into a road and then turns into a highway. When you do something so often, and without regard to the natural world or the hidden ethical problems, you create a path. It might not be the right path, but it still exists and is difficult to deviate from it. Sustainable fashion will become more affordable with time, thereby being more sustainable. It just takes a little inertia, dedication, and time.

Sometimes Eco Friendly is Interchanged with Organic

This is another common misconception when words are used so often that they lose their meaning. Organic means that the clothing produced without the use of pesticides. A pair of polyester yoga pants is technically organic, even though it's not Eco-Friendly.

Therefore, organic is not always sustainable. There needs to be a balance between how it was made, what it was made with, who made it, and who can afford it.

Sometimes people also just use the words Organic and Gluten Free when it comes to clothing. Sometimes Organic cotton is better for you than conventional materials. However, sometimes the cost is too great that it's not affordable for the everyday person. If you have chemical sensitivity, organic cotton is a godsend, but it is not necessary for everyone.

There are no standards or ratings on Eco Friendly Fashion

Finally, there are really no official standards regulating any of this. I know that there are differences between eco fashion, ethical fashion, and sustainable fashion because I have a degree in Sustainability. Not a lot of people in the sustainability field spend their time looking at the fashion industry. Thus, marketers can simply get away with using any kind of green buzzword without it having any value.

To fix this, we need to be more diligent consumers. However, I know that fashion, and consumerism alone will not let us solve the world's biggest problems. We choose sustainable fashion because it improves our everyday lives and makes us feel better. Starting sustainable fashion businesses can also be a big help for shifting the market. The future of fashion will be full of medium-sized businesses producing amazing sustainable products.

Vaguely Ethical Fashion

Ethical Fashion is a poster-child for the idea that buying things can solve social injustices. Buying more ethically sourced products is a noble cause, but it is not always Sustainable. Here are 5 reasons why ethical fashion is not always sustainable.

Ethical Fashion is a Subcategory of Sustainability

Every square is a rectangle, but not every rectangle is a square. The same logic applies to Ethical Fashion and sustainability. Ethical fashion is a subgroup of sustainability that focuses heavily on social justice, workers rights, and combatting exploitation. These critical issues need to be fixed, but using the word ethical in place of sustainable is simply not true.

The Triple Bottom Line

If a product is truly sustainable, it would have to balance three different factors: Ethics, The Environment, and the Economy. This is called the Triple Bottom Line. Ethical Fashion is definitely a step up from conventional fast fashion. By default, however, it is not automatically sustainable.

If the fashion is Ethically sourced, but pollutes at three times the rate of current fast fashion, whether, through imports, sourcing, transportation, or disposal, it is not environmentally friendly. Therefore, it is not sustainable.

Ethical Fashion is not Always Affordable

If the fashion is both Ethically sourced *and* Environmentally Friendly, but not affordable, it is not sustainable. Sustainable materials and supply chains are simply not always there, thus driving up costs.

We sometimes confuse affordability with extravagance when it comes to fashion because of the fast fashion culture. Comparable to modern day times, a woman in 1900 owned about thirty garments total, compared to the (generous) average of over 108 per woman today. Dresses in 1900 cost at least $300 when adjusted for inflation. Today, you can get a dress at forever 21 or H&M for less than $5.

We don't Understand True Cost vs Perceived Cost in Ethical Fashion

It is challenging to factor in the true cost of production for a product when a perceived cost is advertised. If you are told that a dress is $15, you just think that it is worth $15. That's a bargain. You don't see the $100's spent on welfare for the below-living wage workers. You don't see the child slaves making pennies per dress. We just see $15, and it's tough to shell out more than that when we simply cannot calculate the damage.

Some ethical fashion may be able to take advantage of this confusion by charging the price of the true cost of the garment that is actually cutting corners. Because we don't have a fair or easy way to quantify environmental damage, along with the lack of education or regulation on what "ethical fashion" even means, there is a distrust in the fashion community.

Sustainable Fashion Needs to be Mainstream

The idea goes back to environmental and ethical products that aren't yet affordable, and therefore unsustainable. The sustainable fashion movement is gradually moving towards ethical-economical-environmental fashion instead of fast fashion.

Affordable products are linked to scalability. Like any business or idea, if you cannot scale the production to meet the needs of demand, company, or idea will flounder or stagnate. Sustainable fashion will not be sustainable until it is affordable. It cannot be affordable until we have enough companies sizing up profitable production of ethical-environmental products at a low cost.

Companies cannot size up production until the public shows an interest in sustainable fashion, and they cannot do that until sustainable fashion is not more affordable. You see the catch 22?

Sustainable Fashion Means More Mindful Systems

So to fix this, we need to embrace the true cost production instead of perceived cost production. We need to raise awareness on the importance and inevitability of sustainable fashion. Mainstream companies need to see that charging more for sustainable products will be profitable over time than the current fast-fashion trend. We need to embrace minimalist fashion and slower style to stop buying so much and focus on the things that matter.

Affordable Sustainable Fashion

Affordable sustainable fashion are words that don't seem to make sense together. With today's trends, sustainable fashion seems Uber to be expensive. Why pay $100 for a sustainable shirt when you can get the same shirt for $25. It looks like a scam.

We have an idea of what sustainable fashion is, but sometimes it's not always true. Sustainable fashion by default is affordable and here are three reasons.

We are used to Fast Fashion prices

It is tough to justify buying something that seems so expensive when you can buy cheap, trendy clothing and then just replace them every year.

Many of us would rather buy something cheap and easy every year to look trendy, or in the IN crowd. It starts in High school when we are constantly growing out of clothing and want to look our best because we want to impress our classmates.

Once we graduate, we still seem hooked on fast fashion because it is simply there, familiar, and cheap. We get comfortable with the prices and the amount of clothing in our closets. It doesn't always have to be this way.

Therefore, when we see the real cost reflected in a product, we see it as an exorbitant cost because so many things are not accounted for in the cost of fast fashion. Companies get away with it because we feel like we can't do anything.

Once we start becoming more comfortable with higher prices for truly sustainable clothing, will we start to see them as more affordable?

We are used to buying way more than we need

That last sentence kind of seemed like an oxymoron. How could someone become comfortable with spending more on clothes and possibly be more affordable than buying cheap fast fashion?

Simple: we have too much clothing

So many minimalist bloggers have popped up in the last five years, and it seems like a farce. I worked hard for my things. Why should I give them up?

It's not necessarily about getting rid of things or finding some ideal level of perfection by living as minimally as possible. It's mostly about living our best lives with as little burden as possible.

We don't have to throw away all our clothing and replace it with 5 super expensive articles of clothing that we wear all day and every day. It's about realizing that we need to invest more in fewer articles of clothing.

I had 10 pairs of shoes (and that's pretty moderate for some people I know), and I only ever wore 2. They all wore out constantly, and I was left replacing them every year.

If I spent $30 per pair and had 10 pairs, I'd be spending about $300 every year. Vs. I could spend $200 on two pairs of shoes that go with everything and would last at least 5 years. $1,500 vs. $200? I'll take the $200.

But we don't even want to think about that kind of math most of the time because this pair of shoes is adorable, and I need it, and I can only afford $30 this month.

Until we take a good hard look at ourselves, the outrageous cost of fast fashion will seem more affordable than genuine affordable, sustainable fashion.

Affordable sustainable fashion isn't mainstream

There's a fancy economic way to describe this, but basically: the more of something you make, the cheaper it is to make. Most fast fashion prices are so low, not just because they use basically slave labor. It's also about scalability. Ford didn't invent the automobile. He invented the assembly line which dramatically cut down the cost of producing cars.

The same goes for affordable, sustainable fashion. Many new companies end up on the higher end of the price point because they are on such a low scale of production.

You don't have to treat your workers like garbage to still have an assembly line.

Affordable, sustainable fashion will become more mainstream when we can make more. We will make more, once companies see that it's profitable to produce more. Companies will see the profitability once we, as consumers, demand products and sway the companies to invest more.

Slower Style – The Amazing Future of Sustainable Fashion

Shopping More Sustainably

Supporting the Causes You Care About

Slower Style – The Amazing Future of Sustainable Fashion

Can Fashion Stop Climate Change?

It seems ridiculous to ask how can fashion stop climate change. There are so many factors at play. Fashion is seemed as frivolous. Don't you think it's big oil that is at fault here? Well not exactly. This article talks about how big the fashion industry is, and what it can do to play a vital role in solving climate change.

So, can fashion actually stop climate change?

The short answer is no. At least not alone. If you took a pizza and divided it up into the industries responsible for climate change, it wouldn't even be a shoestring width, let alone a meal.

When I graduated with my degree in sustainability, a lot of people were disappointed that I didn't go right away to grad school or start working for some government organization to help stop climate change. I might be a climate scientist, but the work didn't make me happy. I realized that there were other ways that we can advocate change for sustainable practices. Fashion is a majorly underserved sustainability niche. It makes me happy, and if somehow we can make a change in this industry, we are likely to be a part of a much larger movement.

I realized that there were other ways that we can advocate change for sustainable practices. Will fashion stop climate change? Not alone, but here are 3 reasons why it will definitely help:

Fashion is a Change Maker for Other Industries

Old men in their stuffy suits are usually quick to scoff at the fashion industry for asserting that they can produce change for larger social issues. Through Alexa Chung's British Vogue series on the future of fashion, she meets with many changemakers within the industry.

During this one set, she meets with social change makers within the fashion industry. Sure, they focus more on the topic of feminism, but we can understand that fashion as a whole can influence change in many other industries.

Through this understanding of how fashion influences our culture, it is not difficult to see how eco-fashion and other sustainable trends are going to influence the industry in the next 5-30 years. People who believe otherwise will simply be on the wrong end of history.

We are Always Going to Need Clothing

Simply put, we are always going to need clothing. Unless of course, we all collectively embrace nudity or ascend to a higher plane of existence. But for now, and at least the next 100 years, we can see that clothing is a necessity. Fashion dictates clothing. It helps us express our emotions and compensate for our first impressions.

With the influencing power of the larger economy at stake, fashion is going to be a forerunner in the sustainability movement. The two biggest issues that the industry faces is in ethical labor and using ecologically friendly materials without being too expensive. Yes, it is possible to change. It just requires a little bit of collective effort, and we will get there.

Fashion has Influenced over our Spending Habits

We are not going to buy our way out of climate change. However, there are other factors at play to determine the market other than our spending habits. Executives, Investors, and the people with the money and power use our spending habits as a gauge on what people want. Sure, buying an organic cotton tee shirt for $5 or more won't make you change the world... And yet.

The more that we change our spending habits, the more that our actions will be amplified through these trends. Businesses base decisions off business trends. The total

US organic sales and growth over the past ten years has doubled by over 20 billion dollars which is huge.

We can't dismiss this trend due at least in part by the sustainable movement, and in turn the fashion industry. Influence is not easily measured, but spending habits are more influencing than what we might like to believe on the surface.

Celebrity Endorsement Overlaps with Activism

One day, decades ago Al Gore took the stage to talk about an Inconvenient Truth. It started a chain reaction of celebrity activism to help stop climate change. Ever since we have been inundated with messages from celebrities (on both sides of the political divide) to help prevent climate change. The fashion industry is no different.

Celebrities like Gwyneth Paltrow, advocate greener living through conscious spending. Right now, there might be resentment towards "green" products from people who don't believe in climate change. If they hear about the functionality of a product or have a celebrity endorsement, they're on board. Appeal to guilt doesn't always work for climate change. If we are somehow reducing our impact, even if we don't know about it, it's a win-win.

So the big question: Can Fashion Stop Climate Change? Maybe, but not in a way that you expect.

Sustainable Fashion Mistakes

It's discouraging to see my friends make these sustainable fashion mistakes. I decided to set the record straight by listing the top five sustainable fashion mistakes and how to fix them.

Buying A More "Sustainable Alternative" Duplicate

This is the most common out of all the other sustainable fashion mistakes. My life isn't green enough, so I should replace all my not so green things with more green things.

The problem is that many clothes you have are just fine. There's this thing in economics called a sunk cost. You already have three *cough* twenty *cough* purses or shoes, but you need to buy just one more because it's green. Stop right there.

A lot of things you have are just as fine. Focus more on what you have and practice minimalism in your wardrobe. Stick to a style plan, and repurpose or give away all the things you aren't going to use.

Covering Up Your Sustainable Fashion Mistakes by Purchasing More Unsustainable Clothing

This is slightly different than other sustainable fashion mistakes. This time, you aren't quenching your guilt for the environment by purchasing more sustainable alternatives to the clothes you already have. Instead, you are so full of guilt that you break down and spend $500 at Zara for a bunch of "cute" clothes you don't need.

Guilt is a fickle emotion. Sometimes, when we have too much of it, we develop this belief that we aren't good enough and we will never be good enough. I like to call this the forget about it all mentality. Fashion is no different. Try to keep your guilt in check by realizing that you can't fix everything, but you can do some things. Balance is key. Put down that credit card. Breathe!

Going for Things That Are Simply Labeled "Eco Friendly"

We are all admittedly lazy by default. When we want to invest in eco friendly clothing, it is easy to take a simple way out and just buy clothing that is labeled as Eco

Friendly. Understand that by default, "Eco Friendly" is not always "Sustainable."

Sustainability is the balance between
people, the planet, and the economy.

Not everything that is eco-friendly is good for the rights of workers, or is carbon neutral, or even economically viable. It is not a regulated word. Marketers can put eco-friendly on virtually anything, and can sometimes just flat-out lie.

To avoid this, realize that sustainability is a slow process and is not something we can buy ourselves out of. There is really not a lot you can do on a personal level to stop climate change or influence collective decisions through your purchasing habits.

Instead, focus on your own experience and how clothes make you feel. Buy less. Buy better. Research your Products. Have a solid Style Plan. Stick to your Fashion Goals. Don't follow the trends for the sake of them being trends. Don't forget to Breathe.

Going for the Cheap but Greener Option

The goal you should have in mind with sustainable fashion is quality over quantity. Green junk is still junk... even if it's made from bamboo instead of plastic.

Sustainable fashion is rooted in minimalism and anti-consumerism. If you need to buy something, you're better off buying something of higher quality that will last a while than buying many things that are slightly better for the environment. Buying many things consumes more resources than just buying one good thing, even if it has a slightly higher carbon footprint and slightly more expensive.

Not Having a Plan for your Wardrobe

Many people make sustainable fashion mistakes when they rely on impulse purchases. It doesn't matter if it's slightly more eco-friendly or made out of locally sourced, fair trade, organic cotton produced by fair-wage workers. If it doesn't go with the rest of your outfits, you are never going to wear it, and it might as well not have been purchased at all.

Focus instead on minimizing your wardrobe to a few staple pieces and then replace your staple pieces with more sustainable options when they wear out. When I started Bottle Thread, I wanted to have a shirt that would last me a long time, and go with everything. I didn't start out saying oh wait, how can I make a sustainable fashion company? I had a problem, and couldn't find a solution anywhere, so I made my own, and now it's success.

Sustainability starts with solving long-term problems, not bandaging short term "eco-friendly" solutions. Remember that when you buy anything or start any business.

Minimalism

Minimal Chic is the new IT girl. Fashion seems to be the last thing on people's minds when they think about sustainability, but it's in every part of our lives. We wear clothing every day. We want to look our best. Why not save time, energy and resources by being a little more minimal.

A staple denim. Sandals. A dress. A bag that goes with everything. Find a way to mix these things into your wardrobe, and you'll be saving money as well as keeping waste from landfills.

Match Closet Items that Go With Everything Else

The best way to reduce your clothing waste is to pick items that specifically go together with everything else. If you can't picture wearing it more than once, do not buy it. Simple.

For this outfit, I chose a basic denim jacket. I personally do not like ripped clothing. It just makes it look cheap and wasteful. A solid denim jacket will serve you for at least three seasons out of the year and goes with literally everything.

Monochromes are Minimal Chic

The easiest thing when it comes to clothing is to get caught up in is color matching. With so many colors and textures, in addition to types of fabric and quality, it could easily drive a person insane. Instead, why not take away some of those needless choices by sticking to a color palette that works for your style.

I'm not saying everyone should go 100% monochrome black and white. Though if you did, you could look posh AF. The key here is to use less and stick to a color scheme that suits you.

Dresses never go out of style. You can mix it with so many things. Grey looks good on anyone. Definitely a staple piece.

Shoes are an Asset, not an Accessory

Shoes are my frienemy. I love them and hate them at the same time, so I developed a system to make sure I don't have more shoes than I need (even though I still love so many kinds.) Find a solid pair of shoe that you could see yourself wearing every day.

A solid pair is an asset. Don't make shoes your accessories.

Invest in Quality, not Quantity

Sage advice and the center of minimal chic. There are so many hidden costs to cheap fashion; it's frankly not worth it. If you can, you're better off investing in a solid purse that goes with every outfit instead of owning 30 purses that only in part, or not at all go with everything in your closet.

I personally adore Kate Spade purses, while I find some others tacky. I'd rather spend $300 on a solid purse or two that lasts for over 20 years than buy a new purse every year for $50 each. $600 vs. $2500. I think that math is pretty clear.

Sustainable Fabrics

Sustainable Fabric is a touchy subject. You can't go to a store and look at a label and see that the garment was made with 100% sustainable material. It's frankly too much to ask of a product because there is simply no way to judge if a fabric is sustainable or not. Instead, I am going to break down the different types of sustainable fabrics, what each of them actually does, what to look out for, and it's sustainability

Organic Cotton

Organic cotton is a prime sustainable fabric. Practically, anything that is organic is better for the environment. However, even though true organic cotton is a good eco-affordable fabric, it is not always ethical, or eco, therefore not always sustainable. A product needs to consider a lot of different factors for it to be considered sustainable.

Just because it says it's organic cotton doesn't mean that's the whole story. As I explain in my sustainable business list, companies may focus more on eco or ethical sides of things but not the other. There have to be a lot more factors in play instead of it just being organic. However, true organic cotton is pretty sustainable as a whole.

Recycled Polyester

Recycled polyester is my personal favorite sustainable fabric because of its versatility and renewability. I started Bottle Thread on the premise that we can turn recycled bottles into a wrinkle-free fabric, and I still stand by that decision. I would prefer to have the products made by an even more renewable, plant-based material. Though, we have all these plastic bottles and nothing to do with them. Making comfortable fashion is a pretty good use, and I'm pretty satisfied with my clothing line so far.

Hemp

Hemp is going to be the next big thing for fashion, and global production as a whole. I haven't gotten too big in hemp yet because I'm still very focused on recycled polyester, but it's on the list. I'll probably end up writing a whole article on Hemp in the next couple of months. Until then, just know that it is a pretty sustainable and versatile fabric as a whole and will be a lot more widely used in the future.

Bamboo

Fabric made out of Bamboo has a lot of sustainable vibes, but just like organic cotton, it may not always be sustainable. Bamboo grows very fast, but we cannot guarantee the working conditions in which it was made, nor the transportation costs in which it traveled to be produced. For this reason, bamboo can be a very sustainable fabric, but not by default.

Vegan

Vegan fabric to me feels like saying the fabric is gluten-free. Some people are vegan for sustainability reasons. Others are vegan out of empathy for animal cruelty, or diet, or a whole bunch of other things. You know what fabric is vegan? Virtually anything and everything from fast fashion. Vegan simply means "no animals," and that is a vast category when it comes to fabric. Therefore, I shouldn't even have to say that vegan isn't always sustainable. Though if you're still into vegan fashion, awesome.

Made in the USA

Made in the USA, or domestically made if you live in another country, is sometimes touted as a sustainable fabric... but again, it isn't always. Like I said about vegan fabric, made in the USA is a broad category, and apparently, it's not always sustainable. Also, things being made overseas aren't inherently bad, I wanted to point that out. Some people prefer USA made fabric to help motivate the local economy.

Trading overseas can be just as sustainable, ethical, and even more affordable than domestic based products. The only really good thing about domestically made fabric is that it cuts down on the carbon footprint.

Fair Trade

Fairtrade fashion is pretty noble of a cause, but alas it is not inherently sustainable. When we talk about fair trade, it falls on the ethical side of sustainability, not inherently eco-friendly or affordable. Fairtrade is most of the time made overseas to help real people in struggling economies. There is a whole certification process to be considered a truly fair trade product. That being said, the transportation emissions and affordability factor may not make fair trade sustainable by nature.

Small Scale

When I was going through my list of sustainable fashion companies, I came across this one brand called "A Wool Story." It was by far the most sustainable brand out of all of them. I don't even think it was their goal. From what I gathered, A Wool Story is a New York Based Brand that turns eco fabrics into ethical hand-made clothing at a pretty affordable rate. Every single company on this list has something that they do better than the others, but I couldn't pin it on this brand. It surpassed the requirements for each of them, and I couldn't think of any problem until I thought of scalability.

See, this is something I didn't take into account of the economic side of sustainability for this list. I was basing it off the affordability for customers, and I haven't thought of a "sustainable business plan." To be a sustainable business and not a non-profit, there needs to be profit and scalability. It must be difficult for the person making these clothes because they are probably not paying themselves the full price that they deserve for the product, which in turns makes it less ethical.

Overall, there needs to be a scalability that matches the rest of the sustainability within a company to make it sustainable. No company is perfect. Each does really well in one regard while lacking in another, and that's okay. Sustainability is not about perfection; it's about balancing and leading to a brighter future.

Organic Fabrics

Organic fabric comes in many varieties, and they are not always sustainable. Here, we look at the different kinds of organic fabric, their benefits, and how sustainable they can be.

Let's start off by talking about sustainable fabric. I wrote a whole other article on sustainable fabric. It's basically fabric that considers the environmental, economic, and ethical impacts of said fabric in regards to how it is produced, advertised and sold.

That being said, just because a fabric is not fully sustainable does not mean it isn't worthwhile. Many fabrics and clothing take into account issues of social justice by paying their workers a living wage. Others lessen the impact of climate change by using renewable resources.

So What Exactly is Organic Fabric?

Organic fabric is slightly different than other types of sustainable fabric. Organic means that a product did not use pesticides while making the said product.

That's pretty much it.

Yes, there is an Organic certification process, and yes, many organic fabrics meet other awesome sustainable milestones: improved environmental health, encouraging biodiversity, reducing the impact on climate change. Though it will not always meet the other factors and we must remember that when shopping for sustainable fabrics.

Now that we've gotten that out of the way, we can now talk about the different kinds of organic fabric and their sustainable impact.

Types of Organic Fabric

If you ever see something that says organic fabric, most of the time what they are saying is true. If it is certified, that would be even better. Though, now and then you might have to check the brand validity to see where it comes from.

Cotton

Cotton is my comfort zone when it comes to organic fabrics. It's relatively cheap compared to the other types of sustainable fabrics. It's relatively easy to grow and is pretty omnipresent in the realm of sustainable fabrics. The conventional cotton fabric is easier to grow in monocultures, which cuts down on the cost of production. As time goes on, it will become even less expensive because of newer, cheaper, sustainable methods of production.

Bamboo

Bamboo is a fabric that is starting to become more popular for its cooling properties, and it increases in production, making it more affordable. Most of the time, it will be organic by default, but as production gets larger, there may be an increase in pesticide use.

Hemp

Hemp is not grown on a massive scale, yet, but it's expected to grow drastically within the next 20 years. Since it's not grown on a massive scale yet, there isn't as much of an issue with monocultures and pests that require pesticides.

Silk

Silk is super luxurious, but also super expensive compared to other fabrics. It is spun using the secretions of the silkworm, primarily produced in East Asia. If you want to go to the silk route and want to save money, you'd be better off practicing minimalism on key wardrobe pieces instead of switching your entire wardrobe.

Wool

Wool is an unsung hero for sportswear. As a mild back-country expert, I rely on wool to last over a week without being washed. When it comes to outdoor adventures cotton = death, and wool = bae. Wool may be a little bit more expensive to handle but is a pretty sustainable fabric.

Some people may be worried about animal welfare rights. I'm concerned as well, but not as much as I value balancing the efficiency between animal rights, people's rights, the planet, and affordability. Sustainability is not about ONE ANSWER IS THE ANSWER TO EVERYTHING, but incorporating as many possible options for as many people as possible. Therefore, wool may not be for you, but it might be for someone else, and that is okay.

Fabric that is TECHNICALLY Organic Fabric

Okay, I like being a little cynical: polyester is technically organic. Why? Because it doesn't involve any pesticides. Is polyester a sustainable fabric? Maybe. Not always. Most of the time NO. Sometimes it is the complete opposite of a sustainable fabric, which is why I like pointing it out.

Virtually, anything that doesn't require pesticides to produce is technically considered organic.

It's like using the word "Natural" – naturally made in a lab by natural humans. The term alone does not guarantee its safety or impact on the environment.

Eco Friendly Fashion

When it comes to sustainable fashion and eco fashions, they are seen interchangeably. This is not entirely true, and it's important to distinguish the two. Here's why:

Eco Fashion Can Ignore Human Rights Violations

Yes, you read that right. Since eco-fashion is sometimes confused with sustainability, it's important to realize that the two are not the same.

Slower Style – The Amazing Future of Sustainable Fashion

Sustainability is the balancing combination between people, the planet, and the environment.

This means that if someone labels their clothing as eco-friendly, they don't have to disclose that child slaves possibly made their products. It's not always the case, but understand that there has to be a triple-bottom-line involved for a company to call themselves sustainable. This is a huge problem.

True Sustainable Fashion is environmentally friendly and does not exploit workers

Understanding sustainable fashion is so essential for consumer habits. We can't fix the world's problems by shopping. We can, however, demand better quality products that aren't destroying the planet or harming the rights of people. An official trade regulation certification does not exist yet for this problem in the realm of fashion. Someday it will and until then, know that true sustainability happens when:

- The product is from an environmentally friendly source
- Workers have safe working conditions and earn a living wage
- The company can make a decent profit
- The garment is affordable

Apparently, there is some gray area with all of these. Sustainable fashion is the tip of the iceberg for a larger society-wide problem of excessive consumerism and over-extraction of natural resources. A wardrobe isn't going to solve that, but it can definitely help.

Someday there will be a much better system for producing and consuming our clothing. The fashion industry will be dominated by medium-sized designers instead of the huge conglomerates. We will get there. Until then, we can focus on buying the best possible garments for their own right.

Vegan Fashion

Cruelty-free fashion falls under the ethical side of sustainable fashion, but that doesn't mean by default that cruelty-free is sustainable.

I kind of sound like a broken record writing about how ethical, eco-friendly, fair-trade and now cruelty-free fashion are all sub-categories of sustainable fashion, but it does not make them sustainable by default.

All are essential steps in their own regard, but the use of these terms interchangeably with each other is diminishing their power and importance.

Cruelty-Free Fashion Is Vaguely Defined

As many of you already know, I am pretty big into Pinterest. Almost all of my boards fall around the different categories of sustainability. Something interesting happened the other day: A post I wrote on eco-fashion ended up on someone's "Cruelty-Free" board.

Don't get me wrong. I love it when people pin my posts to their boards, and I'm not going to tell someone not to do something to the meaning of different words. I could not let this pin go when I realized how ubiquitous the words cruelty-free and sustainability has become.

There needs to be a change, and it starts with understanding.

Cruelty-Free Fashion is a vaguely defined word. There is no regulation on the use of the word. If someone said a pair of gluten-free jeans was LEED certified, the LEED certification would have a lawsuit on their hands, and they'd likely win. Though if someone says something is "sustainable" or "cruelty-free" it's not always the case.

Cruelty-Free Fashion is not Eco-Friendly by default

When it comes to cruelty-free fashion, it falls more on the side of Ethical Fashion and not always Eco Fashion. If a product is made from new plastic, it's not eco-friendly, but can be considered Cruelty Free. This misconception is a problem in the understanding of sustainability and marketing.

The result is a ton of articles and pins that are mixing up terms, relaying false information, and generating mistrust for the entire industry.

Cruelty-free focuses more on the welfare and ethics of animal rights. Sometimes it includes the rights of workers and distributors, but that usually involves another certification.

Many People Still Don't Understand Sustainability, Let Alone Cruelty-Free Fashion

Sustainability is all about the balance between the environment, the economy, and ethics.

With the blogging boom over the past decade, there has been a surge in eco-ethical blogs. On the one hand, I think this is amazing! So many people are now into being sustainable consumers but at a cost. Many sustainability "experts" don't know what they're talking about and many actual sustainability professionals are way too busy to blog.

Terms like Cruelty-Free Fashion may hit well on SEO or Pinterest, but the quality of content for those articles is not usually correct. It is going to take some time, patience, and more experts in the field to sort out the SEO dilemma that is fueling the misinformation across the web.

Some transitions are inevitable, and this will be one of them.

Fair Trade Fashion

Air trade fashion is leading the way regarding ethical consumerism, but it is not always sustainable. This article explains 7 reasons why it's so:

Ethical Fashion Doesn't Have to Be Eco-Friendly

Fair Trade Fashion is for the most part associated with the Ethical side of sustainability. This does not mean, by default that ethical fashion or Fair-Trade Fashion has to be eco-friendly.

Most of the time, consumers may overlook this and simply buy something because they associate ethical with "good" or Eco-Friendly with "good." But simply "good" or "better" than fast fashion doesn't make it automatically sustainable. Calling something sustainable when it does not desensitizes us to its importance.

Sustainable Fashion is Fair Trade, but Fair Trade Fashion Doesn't Have to Be Sustainable

For a product to truly be sustainable, it needs to incorporate three important factors:

The past century has been weighted heavily on the profitability side of the spectrum. The industry itself is not going to automatically switch over to being sustainable out of the goodness of their hearts. It will happen gradually, over time when consumers start demanding the triple bottom line. We will use up resources that make the old way of doing things unaffordable.

Whether or not you are going to profit from this transition is up to you. It's going to happen regardless. Focusing on demanding an only fair trade is looking at the problem from a very narrow point of view.

Fair Trade Fashion Isn't Always Affordable

Fairtrade fashion and fair trade as a whole have been associated with the affluent and liberal elite. The only people who seem interested in purchasing a fair trade garment from 10,000 villages are the same kinds of people who can afford $20 for a slice of quiche. When the median household income in 2016 was $56,000, spending $70 on a dress doesn't seem practical.

Sustainable Fashion will happen when it is mainstream and affordable to buy an eco-friendly garment produced by a person earning a living wage. This future is not too far off. It just takes time, incentives, and innovation.

Fair Trade Fashion Isn't Always Accessible

Going to a fast fashion chain at a local mall or quickly finding the cheapest garment on Amazon is super easy, but looking for affordable, eco-friendly, ethical clothing is hard. Accessibility will happen once big-name companies with the systems have the right incentives to supply more fair-trade products.

H&M, for all their labor wage disputes and contributions to climate change, have been at least trying to recycle old garments through their exchange program.

 You may laugh, thinking that a company so unsustainable as H&M are seeking by on the eco-friendly scale by simply trading in and recycling old clothing. The fact that they are at least trying is a very good sign for sustainability in general because accessibility is linked to being mainstream.

Fair Trade Fashion Is Not Yet Mainstream

See, we need large companies like Zara, H&M, and Forever 21 to make sustainable shifts in their products. These mega companies aren't going anywhere. They have all established a huge network of trust and accessibility among consumers. Their minor shifts towards being more eco-friendly and ethical are enormous compared to similar steps that can be taken by smaller companies.

The little initiatives the trade in program at H&M does is to test the market and see if we are willing to spend slightly more on sustainable clothing. It's called Incrementalism, and it is what shapes the future of fashion and sustainability. Fair Trade Fashion will be mainstream someday when the market (us) demands it. It will happen when workers inevitably rise and demand a higher wage. Fast Fashion companies will have to scramble to find new ways to market their fashion, even if that means marketing slower style at a slightly higher price.

The Fair-Trade Certification may cover the Supplies, but not the Labor

An old conundrum: What exactly about the product is a fair trade? Is it how the fabric was produced or how the garment was made? Usually, it is difficult to tell the difference. Most of the time, companies can get away with charging more for a fair-trade sourced shirt, but it was still made by a worker earning below a living wage. If a customer is not careful in the labels to see that it was also organically sourced, fair trade, and something about how it's carbon neutral, the customer is not getting a "sustainable" product.

But let's be clear, it is difficult for customers, in general, to know how sustainable a product is. While there are steps you can take to be a more responsible consumer, the real change will happen on a much larger scale.

68

The World Fair Trade is Used Interchangeably with "Ethical" and "Sustainable"

Lazy marketing is to blame here. When someone without a sustainability degree talks about how to be more sustainable, it turns into a mess of buzzwords. Most marketers don't know what they're talking about regarding ethical and eco-friendly. We basically just let them get away with it because there are no regulations on using the word sustainable. If a marketer said that their gluten-free pants are LEED certified, there would be a lawsuit in false advertising.

The words sustainable and ethical are tough to certify because they are used so ubiquitously. Instead, consumers are going to rely on third-party certifications to understand even what is going on. Though relying on third-party certification is difficult, and too much to ask from consumers. Just understand that over time, these things will change. The only things you can do are basically trying to feel better and maybe call your elected officials.

What we Can Actually Do

It sucks to feel like things are out of your control, mainly when you care so much. The most rewarding thing I have done is to start my own fashion sustainable company to address these issues on a smaller local scale. The future is medium because small to medium-sized companies will lead it. There is a great opportunity for business owners and fashion designers to shape the industry, but only through education and understanding.

69

Saving Money on Sustainable Fashion

Sustainably fashionable people are not always made of money. They simply follow a formula to reduce their waste and wear clothing that suits them best. Here are 10 ways to be sustainable fashionable on a budget.

Understand that Less is More

Sustainability is the balance between people, the planet, and the environment. It's not all about being "eco-friendly." Most of the time, it's a useless buzzword. So, counteract your spending habits to be more sustainable fashionable. You can't change everything that is wrong with the world, but you can do some things to make yourself a more thoughtful consumer.

To do this, realize that less is more. Follow minimalists movements. Reduce your clutter, and stop buying as much. This will be WAY more sustainable than simply consuming more and more things that are labeled sustainable. It's not a regulated term, so you have to be vigilant towards the mentality, and not the advertising.

Wear Clothing that Fits

I see this on both ends of the spectrum. People buy clothing that they WANT to look good in, and not just because they DO look good in it. There is a clear difference. Nothing wastes more of your time towards being sustainably fashionable than buying clothing that doesn't fit. You'll never wear it. Stop kidding yourself.

So many people in my mom's generation hoard all their favorite clothing from the 80's to wear once they lose weight. If this sounds like you then stop and think: Even if I was the same size I was when I was 20, would I still want to wear clothing that has been dated by 30-40 years ago? Yes, some styles remain, but for the most part, you'll want to buy new clothing.

I'm sorry mom; shoulder pads are never coming back!

Know what is in Your Closet

When I was looking for an apartment, I was amazed at the sizes of some of the closet I was looking at. A walk-in closet was the difference between $300/month in rent in some places. I was appalled. Even as a fashion designer, I only own like 50 garments total.

We have so much closet space, and so many garments, that we never stop to think what is actually in our closet. Knowing what is in your closet will allow you to know what you actually need, so you can stop buying duplicates of things you already have.

Eliminate Clothing You Know You'll Never Wear

When I started paring down my closet, I donated over 100 tee shirts to the goodwill. None of them I actually wore more than once. I'm sure many of you have similar amounts of clothing just waiting to be set free. The fashionably sustainable know what is in their closet, and keep a tight monitoring on what goes with what. If it doesn't go with anything, then it's time to give it away.

Visualize Yourself As More Sustainably Fashionable

You need an action plan of what style you will feel to be the best on a daily basis. To do this, start picturing yourself in different scenarios with different kinds of clothing. If you're a bookworm like me, a big cozy sweater makes a lot more sense than a crop-top. I will never wear a crop-top, so why fool myself.

Come Up With a Style Game Plan

Fashion is secretly a math. No one ever tells you this, but it's the secret to being more sustainably fashionable. There are basic math formulas to what looks good with what. It's actually really simple, but once you realize how this works, it will take up your fashion game 10 fold.

Purchase Clothing that You Know You Will Wear in Many Ways

This is minimalist fashion 101, but it applies so well to the sustainably fashionable. Buying and using garments that go with other garments in your closet will allow you to reduce your overall spending. When you reduce your spending cycle, you are a lot more sustainable than speeding up your spending cycle with slightly more sustainable options. Look for quality. Look for things that match your style. Don't buy things simply because they are just attractive.

Slow Down Your Spending Cycle

To slow down your spending cycle, take a good, hard look and be prepared for a reality check. To reduce your shopping habits, it is good to take a step back and realize why you are purchasing things in the first place. 9 times out of 10, when you impulse buy it is because you feel bad about something else in your life.

Practice Mindfulness of the Things You Buy

To combat all of these natural tendencies towards impulse purchases, it's important to practice mindfulness. Understanding that you buy things in response to emotional unrest is a huge step towards being more sustainably fashionable. It also makes you a better person in general.

Slower Style – The Amazing Future of Sustainable Fashion

If you are the kind of person who goes to the mall on a weekly basis and buys a new article of clothing every week, that is 52 articles of clothing you most likely do not need every single year. Going to the mall is okay. Buying things is okay. Enjoying fashion is okay. Being more mindful will keep you from making bad decisions, wasting money, and hurting the planet.

Research Research Research

I rarely buy clothing in stores anymore, to be honest. On the one hand, it sucks because I am not able to feel the clothing or try it on. I also don't get that personal satisfaction of wearing a piece and then immediately buying it to take home. However, online shopping gives me a tremendous advantage on finding a wider variety of clothing that I know exactly where it came from. Once in-person stores, will be able to do that, it will be my own personal heaven.

Until then, research as much as you can of where you are buying your clothing. It'll help you make the best possible decision, and generally save money on more sustainable fashion.

Creating a Sustainable Fashion Business

Becoming a Change Maker

Why is it so Hard for Women to Find a Simple Fitted Button Down Shirt?

A simple fitted button down shirt is hard to find. A couple of months ago, I was reading an article about an MIT grad who made the company Third Love and the "perfect fit bra." In the article, the CEO talked about how many parts go into making a bra, while making a shirt has four pieces of fabric. She was not talking about a simple fitted button-down shirt.

I use the term "simple" loosely. A mark of good editing is when you don't see all the effort and time that goes into the final product. Fashion is no different. So why is it so hard for a woman to find a simple fitted button-down shirt?

Prepare to be unsurprised.

The Simple Fitted Button Down Shirt was created for men over 100 years ago

With the now common intermingling of work and life balance, women in the workforce, and minimalism, the simple fitted button down shirt is now a staple everyday garment for women. It wasn't always this way. Even though the simple fitted button-down shirt seems like it's style has been around forever. Now that it's here, we simply haven't updated the design to meet our needs.

After a long time searching for the right shirt, I simply gave up and decided to make my own. This was the start of Bottle Thread, which is doing pretty well so far. I wanted to make something that would address these issues and was frankly surprised that none of this had been addressed before now.

Cotton is Actually the Worst

During my last reincarnation, I was the female equivalent of a Super Eagle Scout and spent a lot of time camping. One of the universal gear tips is that cotton = death. I'm a fan of cotton clothing, but not for garments you often wear, especially outside.

Non-cotton shirts have to be done the right way, which is why I insisted on higher quality fabric. It just so happens to be made out of recycled bottles.

Stretch is not a priority

Again, the simple fitted button down shirt was made for men to work in the office. It was not made for women, and not made for the everyday activities that we are using them for today.

Cotton, by nature, doesn't stretch much. Some shirts have the elaborate bunching and folding systems in the back that gives the shirt a little bit more. Overall, though it doesn't work well. The beauty of wearing high-quality.

Lazy Sizing

When I was first pitching my idea for Bottle Thread, I had a vastly different reaction based on the gender of my potential investor. Men were dismissive while the women were ecstatic. The Simple Fitted Button Down Shirt was created for men. Men don't er, have large chests and smaller stomachs.

Most button-down shirts for women are basically unflattering tents. The only way to solve this is through using a better fabric and a different sizing system. When I was meeting with one of my advisors, they made an off the cuff comment about using bra sizes instead of the unreliable S-M-L scale.

While I would love it for people to buy more of my shirts, I know this is a big problem that a majority of women face. I would like to see more of my fellow fashion designers solving issues instead of just creating designs for the sake of getting more attention to their brand.

In an industry where attention is the primary metric for profit, maybe doing something a little bit more practical will start to cause a change.

Slower Style – The Amazing Future of Sustainable Fashion

Why I Make Shirts Out of Bottles

When I first heard that it was possible to make my first clothing line out of recycled plastic bottles, I was over the moon. Not just because I was a sustainability major and all the things I learned in my degree were finally coming together. I was finally able to make a viable, breathable, comfortable product... And I would eventually have the travel shirt of my dreams.

Why Bottle Thread Clothing is Made out of Recycled Plastic Bottles:

Recycled Polyester or Polyester made from recycled plastic bottles, is not a new concept. It is mainly used in athletic wear and leisure wear because we tend to

82

associate it with lesser quality. Bottle Thread is changing those perceptions by turning them into minimalist casual-formal wear for when you want to travel or run errands while still looking nice. Here is the rationale behind why I chose my clothing line to be made out of recycled plastic bottles.

Recycled Plastic Bottles are Way More Sustainable

When we talk about sustainability, I'm referring to balancing the environment with the economy and ethics of production. I could have easily just used a polyester fabric or made the shirt abroad... but for real, the cost of production would have only been $5 per unit or less.

We're taking plastic bottles out of the oceans and turning them into comfy, minimalist fashion. I pay my employees a living wage. The company is profitable, and I can scale it like a traditional business. If other big companies should follow my footsteps, then it will be awesome. I just want better fashion and was tired of not being able to find it on my own.

The Shirt is Way More Comfortable

Have you felt a plain white button-down shirt lately? They are scratchy, y'all! The limits of technology make it hard for me to convey just how comfortable this shirt is without letting you feel it for yourself. One of my friends said it was like if a cloud hugged a pile of silk. I'm not sure how that translates, but I am pleased with the product.

It Actually Fits People

The fit of the shirt is just another extension of how comfortable the shirt is. I was tired of baggy "boyfriend" clothes that fashion labels think we want to keep buying. I am not a twig. I have a figure, so do many MANY other women. Where is all the good fitting clothing?

I was pretty selfish when starting this business because I wanted a shirt that could fit me. If other people liked it, awesome.

So the nice part of making this design out of a recycled polyester blend is that it is made to fit better without being baggy. Some shirts try to do this but fail because the shirt gives too much around the chest. That's why I decided to size the women's shirt through relative bra sizes instead of the typical S-M-L scale.

Another thing that I really love is that there is an extra set of invisible "boob buttons" on the women's shirt to make sure everything stays in place without being noticeable. Why has this not been done before? I have no idea.

The Shirt Can Be The Most Minimalist Garment

I was pretty selfish when designing this garment. I wanted something that I can fit into and take with me when I travel (which I'm expecting to be a lot.) I. Hate. Ironing. And never want to do it, so I decided to base the entire clothing line on

a wrinkle resistant, a minimalist garment that (oh by the way...) is sustainable and made from recycled plastic bottles.

It's Very Cost Effective

Getting into some technical details, the cost of labor is pretty expensive in the USA. Though, I am willing to pay more and have it made here because it lowers transportation costs, and minimizes the room for error over a miscommunication.

That being said, using sustainable fabric over traditional cotton on the same design under the same circumstances is still cheaper when we account for labor. Cotton clothing doesn't stretch while the high-quality recycled polyester does. Designers had to create a bunch of convoluted cuts and designs just to make sure a button down shirt "fit" just so.

Because the fabric stretches appropriately, we were able to take out a lot of decorative seam lines, thereby reducing the cost per unit significantly. The overall look is a lot cleaner than it would have been if we went with the traditional cotton approach.

It can easily be made in America

Being a proud citizen, I'm delighted to boast that all the shirts are made in the USA. Yes, this does increase the price to make than if I went abroad, but I believe it is worth it. I wanted to deliver a product that is close to home without sacrificing the quality.

Starting a Sustainable Fashion Company, From Startup to Launch

When it comes to starting your own sustainable fashion line, the idea of going from concept to launch can be very overwhelming. This is because you are focused on the here and now and not over the course of a year. These things take time, which is why this article, as well as my other sustainable fashion business articles, break down these topics into manageable pieces.

Establish Your Own Definition of a Sustainable Fashion Line

So in a broad sense, sustainability is all about the balance between people, the planet, and the economy. When you start a sustainable fashion line, you need to establish what that means for you and your business. Some businesses tend to focus more on the eco side than ethical side while others go for a cheaper product that may not be as eco-friendly as a more expensive product.

Develop your sense of sustainability and reflect it in your clothing line

In the world of a sustainable fashion line, there is no right answer, especially when we are competing against unsustainable businesses on top of competing with each other. Define what is most important to you and try to stick to it. If you build it, they will come. Just try to do your best.

Always Collect New Ideas

This is a piece of advice for not just starting a sustainable fashion business, but for businesses in general, and even life in general. You're going to have an idea that you want to run with, but it might not work with the rest of the ideas and limitations you have. It's okay. Pivot, and move on. Keep collecting new ideas and combining them with other ideas you haven't even thought of before.

Research your System

Entrepreneurs are simply creators of systems. You're going to do your research to make a better system than the one before. I talk a lot about some resources for fashion designers on my other articles. Keep collecting as many resources as possible, so you have them even when you don't need them.

Connect with Helpful People

Collecting resources, connecting ideas, and interacting with other helpful people are key to success in any field. I have my own network of mentors and support groups to get me through a lot of different projects. It's always good to have friends that you can bounce ideas off.

Solve a Problem, Don't Just Stand Out

Many new business owners make the mistake of creating something just for the sake of creating it... not necessarily to solve a problem. If you don't solve a problem, you have to rely on making a problem just to fix it or continually marketing to people to make them feel like they will have a problem if they don't buy your product.

Going into the business mindset with a problem and a solution in mind will allow you to focus on solving real-life problems that will keep rewarding you.

Communicate Clearly and Assertively

You will need to work with a lot of people to make your sustainable fashion line successful. You're not just going to communicate with your audience, but with the manufacturing, supply, and distribution employees. Save yourself from coming off as unprofessional by communicating clearly and assertively.

Set Hard Deadlines

For similar reasons as above, it's essential to set hard deadlines. I personally struggled with this one because I want to be more optimistic about what can be done in a fixed amount of time. Unless if you give hard deadlines, they will always run over time because other people's priorities are not always your priorities.

Your priorities become more of a priority when you set harder deadlines. However, if they aren't met, you need to be a balanced mixture of forgiving and assertive so they won't keep being misses. Virtually everyone struggles with this, so give yourself a break if it takes more than what you anticipated.

Just. Keep. Uploading.

As the wise Casey Neistat would say: Just. Keep. Uploading.

In this regard, he is talking about making YouTube videos, but it is prime advice for anyone owning a business. There may be some hesitation in making videos of yourself, promoting your image, and selling your products because we are rooted in a society-wide double bind of shame.

If you're successful, you shouldn't have to self-promote, and constantly upload new content, but you need to self-promote and constantly upload new content (and products) to be successful.

We hate people who brag and over promote, yet we feel pity for people who sell themselves short, and there doesn't seem to be an answer. The answer is not a clear-cut one, but to balance between the two extremes.

While it may cause a bit of personal uncertainty and hesitation when you're starting out, it will come in time. Just keep uploading, and creating new things and eventually, something will stick.

Stick to Your Core Values

Speaking of sticking, it's essential to maintain a set of core values over the years that it will take for you to reach your dreams. Whether it is starting a sustainable fashion line or any other kind of business. I can guarantee that your vision of success will not pan out exactly as you picture it now. You will need to pivot, and if not, you aren't dreaming big enough. Through all that, you should identify your core values and stick to them from the beginning.

Never Be Afraid to Ask for Help or Criticism

As Elon Musk would say "Constantly seek criticism. A well thought out critique of whatever you're doing is as valuable as gold." Help and criticism are touchy subjects for a lot of people. Instead of feeling less than adequate that you need help, or cringe at any kind of criticism, realize that receiving help and criticisms are the best ways you will grow.

Through all these bits of advice, I know it is not a clear-cut answer on how to start a sustainable fashion line. However, if you keep these principles in mind, you will be able to develop your own sustainable fashion line independent of anything that has been done before. By doing so, you will be immune to copycats, and not be stuck following in someone else's footsteps.

Where to Even Find Sustainable Fashion Manufactures

Finding good sustainable fashion suppliers is one of the hardest parts of starting a fashion line. It took me about three months to figure this part of the equation out. With the help of this article, you can research and locate your perfect supplier within a couple of hours and a few phone calls. I honestly wish I could find an article about this a year ago, which is why I'm writing it. So let's get started:

Determine Your Ideal Manufacturing Country or Region

There are plenty of manufacturers in every country around the world. When you look at the perks and drawbacks of each company, you're going to need to look at specific regions or countries.

First, I started my manufacturing search by calling foreign embassies and basically getting nowhere. I heard that Vietnam and Taiwan had some pretty good sustainable clothing production facilities, but could not find any leads. I ended up calling their embassies, as well as the Chinese-American Embassy in San Francisco to look for someone to point me in the right direction.

The problem with this approach is that the Embassies are usually so busy with other issues that they won't take the time to release any information (mainly, to little people like me). Vietnam was able to send me a spreadsheet with names of companies, but most of them were out of business, and I would have had to hire a translator in order just to make a simple phone call. There had to be a better way.

I decided to go the American way when I realized that it would just make my supply chain a lot easier, and I don't regret it for a second. Sure, the pricing may be a bit higher, but that just means you are creating a higher-value product that can be sold for more in retail.

Research Manufacturers Online

This part took the absolute longest because I couldn't find any leads, even in my own country. A handful of people makes most of the decisions of the production products we buy. In the industry, information is kept pretty close to the vest.

I was about to lose my mind when one day, I was lucky enough to overhear a conversation at the local library.

Another woman was asking the librarian about children's clothing manufacturers. Did. not. even. cross. my. mind. The local library is FULL of online databases with all this information. It was absolutely glorious, how easy it was to find manufacturers both domestic and overseas.

Another great resource is Thomasnet where I ended up finding my manufacturer. They focus more on industrial parts, but there is a pretty substantial directory of clothing manufacturers. Keep in mind, Thomasnet is only in the United States, and some parts of Canada. Wonderful resource. Not all of them are sustainable fashion suppliers, but it's a start.

Look for Minimum Order Quantities

Next, I had to narrow down my list and spend a couple of hours calling different places. I had a list of about 30 places and ended up calling almost all of them. Most were out of business, or shut down in a couple of months and didn't want any new customers. A great question to ask on the first phone call is about minimum order quantities.

Many places have a ballpark range of $10,000. Don't be frightened if you don't have the money right away. This is time for you to do your research and find the right place for your product. Some places, like Indie Source (which is where I started) have a minimum of 300 garments which could be substantially less with a price point of less than $30 per garment.

If you go overseas and can overcome the language barrier, you are greatly increasing your economic potential. Some places in China will produce a small handful of garments for a much lower cost, so you don't have to worry about large order quantities right up front. It's a little bit more of a gray area for "sustainable," though which is why I wasn't into it.

Find Sustainable Fashion Suppliers That Offer Product Development Packages

A great service for start-ups is a product development package that certain manufacturers offer. Not all of them do, which is why you sometimes need the full design CAD models up front for them to take you. I am not a fashion designer. I can sew things, but I have absolutely no experience creating a design from scratch. If you are like me, you will need some help.

Development costs go from anywhere around $1,000 per design to approx $5,000 for a collection. You get full CAD models and real-time samples depending on the service. JUST MAKE SURE that you sign an operating agreement before you send any money. In the operating agreement, it determines that you have FULL OWNERSHIP of the design. Without this, literally, anyone can rip off your design and sell it. I mean, they could do it anyway, but at least you have a legal recourse in case you'll need it later.

When it comes to sustainable fashion suppliers, there WILL most likely be some unexpected costs when developing these designs. It is imperative that you find a way to establish at least a little start-up capital. If you don't have it at first, it's not the end of the world.

Reaching Out to New Freelancers

When you call sustainable manufacturers for the first time, it is pretty intimidating. Here is a 5 step guide of what kinds of questions you should ask.

Ask: Are You Taking New Clients?

The first and most important thing when you call sustainable manufacturers is to ask if they are taking on any new clients. You don't want to be halfway through a conversation when you find out that all their client bookings are full. One time, I reached out to a place in North Carolina thinking that since the business has been around for a while, they would be reliable. Even before we started having a conversation, the receptionist just blatantly stated that they were shutting down within a month and weren't taking on any new clients.

If this happens to you, just be polite. You should have a list of at least 15 places you want to call before even picking up the phone, anyway. I never understood the need to be angry in such situations. When you call sustainable manufacturers for the first time, you want to be professional, and sound like you know what you're doing, even if you don't feel that way.

Figure Out Pricing Minimums

Usually, you will want to ask something along the lines of minimum purchasing order. Most places will let you know right off the bat what their minimum purchasing order is. When you call sustainable manufacturers for the first time, you are essentially setting up a relationship with this company. You want to sound like you know what you are talking about, so they don't feel the need to take advantage of you. This is especially important if you go overseas for your manufacturing because of the language barrier.

Find Out if They Have Design Services

In theory, I could have designed the shirt myself, but why micromanage when you can simply hire out design services for a reasonable cost. Not all places do this, which is why it's important to ask. If they say no, and you don't know what you're doing, it's not the end of the world. There are plenty of 3rd party design services you can find.

If you find a company that doesn't do design services, but it still seems like a pretty decent company to design your clothing line, it's okay to keep looking. Most of the people answering the phone at these places may get several inquiries through the course of the day. If you end up not going with them, it's fine. If you do, it's fine. Maybe, you don't feel comfortable talking on the phone. In this case, do what the experts say, and fake it till you make it.

Be able to Conceptualize Your Idea, and Prepare Reference Samples BEFORE you Call Sustainable Manufacturers

When I first started out with Bottle Thread, It didn't even have a name. I wanted to create a shirt that was super comfortable, fit me well, and wouldn't wrinkle. Since I couldn't find it anywhere on the market, I had to reference some cotton shirts that were already in my closet. I didn't have a men's version of the shirt, so I ended up borrowing one from a friend before realizing how long it would take to get done. Don't make my mistakes. Be prepared to part with them for about 6 months while the designs are being completed.

If you don't have a shirt right away and don't have nice friends who are willing to let you borrow their clothing for such an extended period, then you can always drop approximately $30 on a new shirt from a fast-fashion store. To be a little more sustainable here, you'd be better off finding something from a thrift store. Just make sure you have something you don't mind being without for a little while. Trust me, the payoff at the end will be worth it.

Know What to Say When You Call Sustainable Manufacturers

Nothing is more embarrassing than stumbling over yourself with uncertainty over the phone. I had to rewrite my script about 5 times the first time I reached out to call sustainable manufacturers. Trust me; it gets easier. And remember, even when you think you found the perfect place, call at least 5 more places just to be sure you're getting a good deal.

I want to make sure that you have a successful phone call, here is a quick sheet to keep with you while on the phone:

"Hi my name is _____, and I'm the brand manager for ___ (come up with a name) I'm looking to talk to someone about manufacturing _____(the type of garment)."

- Do you do this, and are you taking on any new clients?
- Describe the garment a little... See if they can make it
- What are your order minimums?
- Do you have product design services?
- What is the order minimum for those services?
- "Wow, this all is exciting. I'm still checking around and need to talk with management before I can give a final answer. Could I please get an email with all the specs for the project?"

This kind of stuff was honestly the scariest part of starting a sustainable fashion company. We can't fix the industry with a simple phone call, but it's at least a start.

Slower Style – The Amazing Future of Sustainable Fashion

2017 - Frownfelter

Promoting Sustainable Fashion

Letting the Movement Have a Voice

2017 - Frownfelter

Identifying Truly Sustainable Businesses

Truly sustainable fashion is hard to come by. We are bombarded with messages on social media and from friends on what it means to be truly sustainable... and let me tell you, most of them have no idea of what they are talking about.

In a world where anyone can be an expert, if they have a website, ideas, trust, and integrity are becoming more and fuzzier. One of the downsides is no longer being able to determine what is good or "right" when anyone can have an opinion. Sustainability is no different.

Sustainable Fashion is all about the triple bottom line.

It's straightforward to say what isn't truly sustainable fashion, but it frankly gets old after a while. So this article is a comprehensive review of the meaning of truly sustainable fashion.

Truly Sustainable Fashion MUST Be Eco-Friendly

We could get into a whole article about what it means for fashion to be eco-friendly. Many people use eco-friendly and sustainable synonymously. Sustainable fashion must be eco-friendly but eco-friendly fashion is not always sustainable. There needs to be a balance between this factor and other factors, obviously.

Truly Sustainable fashion may not be feasible, on a large scale at this point, but it will get there eventually. Eco-friendliness of a product will be the forefront of the movement. Until then, we should just be careful about the meaning behind eco-friendly.

However, just because these categories fall under the whole eco-friendly category, they don't always fall under the sustainable category. There's a much better comprehensive list of all the eco-friendly companies I can come across here.

The Rights of Workers, Customers, and Community NEED to Be Accounted for

Social justice within truly sustainable fashion is a tricky subject, mainly because people sometimes have a negative or political standpoint on social justice and human rights. I'd rather talk about what social justice for workers, consumers, and community members means for the products we use every day.

There are many different factors and standards when it comes to social justice and creating any kind of fashion line. For the most part, it is generally agreed upon that workers are receiving a fair wage, at least based on their geography. Questions about how workers and customers are treated are essential, as well as the greater community where the product is made, produced and sold.

In all honesty, I don't have all the answers on what exactly constitutes a truly ethical clothing line, because there are so many factors at play.

There are clearly a lot of factors here, though remember that just because a business meets at least one of these categories does not automatically make it sustainable. It'd be easier to say that all of these factors must be met for the fashion to be considered Ethical and Sustainable. Though this is not the case, it is important to be aware of these factors as the sustainable fashion movement gains some steam.

Truly Sustainable Fashion NEEDS to be Affordable to Consumers, and Profitable for Business

Affordability is just as crucial for truly sustainable fashion as eco-friendliness and ethics. This is where the so-called "Liberal Bubble" comes into play. Unless a product is mainstream... as in affordable, it will only be available to "liberal elites." These people have good intentions, but struggle in the realm of social justice for their fellow citizens when it comes to consumer spending.

Some people simply cannot afford to spend $500 on an eco-friendly and ethical product. You can combine all the factors from the previous two categories and still won't produce a sustainable product until you can make it available to a majority of consumers.

See, a bunch of these are great perks of business overall. It is not sustainable if they are incorporated at the expense of the environment or the rights of workers and communities.

The Previous Factors Must be Balanced Effectively

Finally, the last factor that defines truly sustainable fashion is profitability for the company itself. This is the true test of entrepreneurship when it comes to starting new businesses across the board. A business needs to balance all three of these factors without losing money. It's difficult but doable.

For now, this is the main reason why we still have fast fashion, and sustainable fashion isn't mainstream. Currently, there isn't too much of a push in the market, even though there will be several years from now. Though, by then, there will be little opportunity for small companies to grow. Even though sustainable fashion companies are not as profitable as unsustainable companies, the market will shift, and it will shift towards companies that take more sustainable steps now.

Upgrading A Thrift Store

The other day, someone asked me in the comments how thrift stores can be more sustainable. By nature, thrift stores are a lot more sustainable than the typical fast fashion establishment. While making an already pretty sustainable organization even more sustainable seems counterintuitive, there is always room for improvement.

Be Open About the Thrift Stores Business and Policy Practices

Not all thrift stores are created equal. While we assume that all thrift stores are open books about their business practices, some may be more secret and less ethical than others.

I personally refuse to shop/donate/encourage shopping at Goodwill or The Salvation Army because of their deceptive advertising tactics and open hostility towards the LGBT+ Community. You might not care about that, and I understand. Though, the worst thing (PR wise) a company can do in the midst of a scandal... is withholding information.

It makes intuitive sense to withhold information when your organization might be in the midst of a scandal. Less information = Less chance for people to talk about scandal... but the practice of public relations and the study of human nature shows that it may actually exacerbate the issue.

The best thing an organization can do is create a story with as much accurate information to the public as possible. A fish is to water as people are to trust. It's difficult to comprehend how vital it is to our survival until it is gone. Withholding information destroys trust and in turn makes a company economically and ethically unsustainable.

Therefore, no matter your beliefs on a topic, a company giving as much accurate information in the midst of a scandal, is more trustworthy, ethical, and overall more likely to be sustainable.

Have a Burn-Free Policy

Thrift Stores get a LOT of clothing. Most of it never sells. The most common practice of thrift stores, when they don't sell their clothing, is to throw it away, burn it, or donate it to an even more economically underprivileged area. Usually, the third option is always the best. However, it doesn't take into account the policies for the organizations that THEY donate to.

The best policy a company can have is to donate any scrap clothing to recycling mills that take old garments and shred them to make new things. If this isn't already a thing, this is a really good market opportunity for anyone interested.

Designers Need to Focus on Customers

This has nothing to do with thrift stores themselves, and more on the companies that produce clothing in the first place. The larger industry of fast fashion tries to come up with as many designs as possible in any given season. That's why when you're shopping at a fast fashion store, and you find that one garment that -almost- is exactly what you are looking for, you settle on it.

Designers can make a name for themselves by standing out from the rest of the crowd. Standing out = recognition. Recognition = Increased Profits. Though, today, with everyone trying to stand out by "being different." The ones who will stand out, in the end, are the plain ones. That's why I started Bottle Thread. We've reached peak standout, and I wanted to go back to basics.

Hence, a lot of the waste problems cannot be solved by thrift stores. It is, in fact, a Band-Aid to the problem. The problem is the fast-fashion industry, not excess clothing sold at a low price. To solve the fast-fashion problem, we need to look at the designers, and the companies they work for.

We as consumers must demand better clothing, and unfortunately getting all of your clothing at a thrift store may not be doing much to solve the larger problem.

What you can do instead

- Buy new clothing from sustainable clothing brands
- Recycle your old clothing
- Only buy what you can use with multiple outfits
- Have a plan for your wardrobe
- Don't buy on impulse

Though, by far, the best thing you can do for the industry is starting your own sustainable clothing line... or support one that already exists. The problem is not the product, but the system that it is made. If you want to make REAL change, you can do so by creating your own businesses or helping out the ones that are already solving the problems you care about.

Sustainable Fashion Bloggers

As a fashion blogger, can you tell how influential you are in the industry? Blogs are 3rd behind brand websites & retail websites in the online resources which significantly influence people to make a purchase. You possibly know it already when you make use of affiliate links, or you have the close community of the readers, yet it is worth noting again: you're influential.

Most of your efforts as a fashion blogger are more on showing what we purchase and wear and the designers that we love, yet what's our responsibility towards forming a more conscious customer and a more sustainable industry of fashion? Unless you are living under the rock, you're possibly aware of how much waste is going on in retail, clothing being shredded & thrown away rather than donated, concentrate on the quality & low cost over quality, yet might not have thought much that you could do something regarding it. You can.

Sustainable Fashion is all about the triple bottom line.

Sustainability within the entire fashion industry is a crucial concern lately, and it was tackled with a few consistencies among the higher-ups for several years.

Sustainability is all about balancing affordability with ethical and eco-friendly practices. Blogging about this topic can seem pretty confusing, which is why it's important to focus on these three principals in the first place. If you're into turning sustainable fashion into your blogging niche, here are three ideas you could consider:

Purchase the Best Quality that You Could Afford

It means that purchasing some items & taking care of them better, yet in the end, you would be happier for this and hence, would the rest of the Earth. There are a lot of keeping up with & feeling like you need to get the newest thing at all times within the world of fashion blogging, yet that is not reality for many readers. After that, attempt to get by on the budget, need to access the gifted items & require practical ideas and concepts for play and work, not unavoidably the latest.

Sell and Recycle on Your Blog

When you have things you have outgrown, do not like anymore or are simply ready to get rid of, you can have them as a donation, or you can sell them through your blog. Many fashion bloggers have stores that are attached to their blogs & offer things up for sale to their dear readers. It is apparently easier to do together with quality items, but it is an excellent way of connecting together with your valued readers, and you recycle the accessories or clothes you are done with. Please do not insult them through charging anywhere close up to full-price & particularly do not attempt to sell the gifted items.

Purchase Pre-owned

Many great bloggers are making up many of their outfits using secondhand or rifted items. Purchasing items from eBay or through your favorite consignment shop are excellent ways of keeping quality items in circulation and become fresh and innovative with your preferred style. You will; not look like the same with any other fashion blogger, and you would serve as the best example to everyone that style is not all about following the latest trends. But, it is all about being true and brave to see who you are.

Fashion Epilogue

Where to Go From Here

Congratulations on making it this far in the sustainable style book. I hope you enjoyed learning about how to make more sustainable decisions, and ultimately starting a sustainable fashion business.

This book is just one of a series of projects to help people better understand and promote sustainable fashion. This is not the final version of this book, so stay tuned for updates and new tips. I'd love to hear your feedback.

- What are some topics you wish I would go more in depth?
- Where were parts in the book that didn't sit well with you and why?
- What's your favorite part of sustainable fashion?
- If you wanted me to add one more chapter to this book, what would it be, and why?

There is also a sustainable fashion business course I am giving you a 50% off discount because you already purchased the book.

FASHIONBOOK1

And if you are interested in trying some Bottle Thread, here is a 20% off coupon and free shipping on orders over $100.

DAPHNE1

If you enjoyed the book, and want to leave a review, feel free to do so on the Amazon website.

Chao!

Slower Style – The Amazing Future of Sustainable Fashion

Made in the USA
Middletown, DE
11 December 2017